Falling for
PETALS

because relationships are like gardens, you reap what you sow...

r. A. bentinck

FYAPUBLISHING | GEORGETOWN

r. A. bentinck

Copyright © 2020 by r. A. bentinck

All rights reserved. No part of this book may be reproduced or utilized in any form or by any means, electronically or mechanically, including photocopying, recording, or by any information storage or retrieval system, without permission in writing from the Author or Publisher. Inquiries should be addressed to FyaPublishing.

FyaPublishing
95 South Turkeyen,
Georgetown, Guyana.

Falling for PETALS r. A. bentinck
ISBN 978-0-9994445-7-3

Cover design by **r.A. bentinck**
Cover image by **Evie S.@evieshaffer**

First best is falling in love. Second best is being in love. Least best is falling out of love. But any of it is better than never having been in love.
—*MAYA ANGELOU*

Bentinck
Always with Love

Contents

Capturing Attention 1

The Petal Spell 3

Her World 5

Not Enough (my apology) 7

Confessions (freeing feelings) 9

The Hunted 11

The Stranger 13

Tales 15

Butterfly Wisdom 16

Un-See 18

Her World 20

Longer Next Time 22

Falling for Petals 24

Are you Really Ready? 26

Confused 30

Her Exceptional Smiles (for Shakkeene) 32

Beyond Physical Beauty 34

COVID-19 (Lover's Blues) 36

Just Like 38

Sinned 40

Unprepared 42

That Smile 43

On the Dance Floor 44

Morality 46

Window Connections 48

- No Sweet Talkin' 50
- Developing interest 53
- Hooked 55
- When Again 56
- Fugacious 58
- Stars 59
- Her World 60
- Braveheart 62
- Body Heat 64
- Troubled Soul 66
- Turn Me Over 68
- Manhattan Bound 70
- The Guilt Complex 72
- Comfort 74
- Turn Me Over 75
- You 77
- Rhythms of the Night 78
- When I Say I Love You 79
- Transformational 82
- Wishful Thinking 84
- Will You? 86
- Mary Jane 87
- Maintaining Interest 89
- Running on Broken Glass 91
- Transformation 92

Relentless	94
Hardship (Broken Petals)	95
The Holy Ones	97
Broken	100
Not Again!	102
Cooking for You	104
Circumstantial scars	105
Poison Ivy	107
Difficult Days	109
Silent Conversations	112
A Place of Hurt	113
Love's Outlaws	115
The Way it Was	117
Complacency	119
Neglect	120
Frustrated	121
Fleeting Moments	123
In My Dreams	125
Unexplained Tears	127
The Ex-Factor	129
The Selfish Kind	130
Loving the Hurt Away	131
COVID-19 (Lover's Ecstacy)	133
Just Because	135
Listen to Your Woman	137
Moments in Time	141

- Scented Secrets 143
- The Cold War 145
- Troubled Woman 147
- The Cold War 149
- Seasons of Love 151
- Curating Memories 153
- When Memories Calls 155
- Only Love 157
- Over You 159
- The Petal Philosophy 161
- A Ballad for the Broken (to My Sisters with Love) ... 163
- Conflicted 166
- The Long Kiss Goodbye 168
- Try Again 170
- Indelible Hurt 172
- COVID-19 (a lover's regrets) 174
- Courage-less 177
- My Soft-Spoken Princess 179
- Love's Aftertaste 182
- Travelling 184
- One More Time 185
- Of Thorns and Roses 187
- Reaping Stupidity 189
- No Limits 191
- My Weakness 193

Incapably	195
Disbelief	196
Who Else?	197
Move On	199
Moments in Time	201
Pearls of Hurt	203
From One Man to All Women	205
Perceived Value	207
One Night	209
Flying in the Rain	211
Choosing My Memories	212
Split Seconds	213
About The Author	215

Capturing Attention
Giving Into The Allure

"Falling for him would be like cliff diving. It would be either the most exhilarating thing that ever happened to me or the stupidest mistake I'd ever make."

–Hussein Nishah

r. A. bentinck

Falling for petals

The Petal Spell

i saw her smile
from a million miles away
as she approached me.

with the gentlest of embrace
she greeted me
and
with soft lips to my earlobe
she whispered words that
vanquish my fears and blues
and straightaway i fell
under her petal spell.

we spent time in the company
of intellectual conversations
and she captivated
my interest and curiosity.
and gradually i surrendered
to the powers
of her petal spell.

she knows how
to make me smile even in
the most gloomy situations,
she has the Midas effect
on almost everything
she touches in my life.

and just like that
i fell headlong

into her petal spell.

one day
she trusted me
enough with her petals
like she trusted
the butterfly
and
she let me taste her nectar.
ever since that day
i have sunk deeper
in her petal spell.

Her World

i never knew how
easily this visible world could
dissolved into nothingness
until i spent a moment
in her world.

i gazed keenly into the depths
of her engaging eyes
and a whole new world
appeared incrementally,

i got captivated by
her dimpled smiles
and caught up
in a world of sweet possibilities,
i felt her buttery skin
and suddenly
an unfamiliar and exciting rhythm
dominated the left side
of my chest.

she giggled and laughed
and the music she made
took me away
to soothing places
where i tasted and felt
sweet reverie.

she spoke with such
intellectual fluency and

r. A. bentinck

i was bedazzled by
her wittiness,
her analytical prowess,
her insightfulness,
her wealth
of extensive knowledge and
mind absorbing conversation.

i got a whiff
of her natural bouquet
and i had to swiftly bridle
my galloping imagination
and out-of-control emotions.

until today,
i never knew how easy
it was for this complex
and sometimes confusing world
to fade away until
i spent some time
in her world.

Falling for petals

Not Enough (my apology)

until today i was
supremely confident
that i was doing an excellent job
adequately describing what you
have shown me
this far.

but

there is so much more
to say and celebrate
about you,
now i feeling like
my words are not
doing enough
to say exactly what i see in you.
despite how many
dictionaries and thesaurus
i consult
the words will never
match up,
they will never do
real justice to appropriately
depict you.

for the first time
today i have come
to the humbling realisation
that my words will
never do justice

in painting your true portrait.
sigh...
i have now peaceful surrender
to the factual reality that
my pleasant words are
not enough.

you are way beyond
my descriptive capacity.

please forgive me
for falling short.

i gave it the best i had.
my words were just
not enough.

Falling for petals

Confessions (freeing feelings)

every so often they say
confessions are good
for the soul.
so today i got a confession.

these seething emotions
were always there
from the very start:

the instant crush on you,
the lustful yearnings
to be with you,
the petal throbbing
as a result of wanting you,
the imaginary longings,
the multiplicities of fantasies,
the numerous thoughts of things
i want and wanted to
do to with you.

these heated feelings
were there from
the very beginning.

now this opportunistic moment
has created the perfect setting
for me to be bold enough
to tell you how
i have been feeling for so long.
i have always wanted you,

*silently i always admired you
from the corners of my eyes,
i adore your sweet smile,
somehow you always
set my emotions afire
and give wings to my
unfulfilled fantasies.*

its been such a relief
to say all the things
i have been feeling
for ages.
thanks for lending me
your listening ears.

the wise often say
every so often
confessions are good
for the soul.
*now that i have confessed
to you,
what are you going to do
about all of my confessions?*

Falling for petals

The Hunted

she hid under the cover
of the dim disco lights
in the darkest part
of the room.
i didn't know
she was digesting
my every dance move.

in the midst of
my perspiration break
she emerged with
laser eyes
and fixed intentions.

she beckons me with
her tease finger
and i was drawn like
steel to a magnet.

my girl was off
to a restroom break
and i know she wasn't
going to be pleased
with the whispered words
that seeped into my ears
from this strange woman
with lips of temptation.

take her home,
and don't run,

r. A. bentinck

walk baby,
it will be here
when you get back
all of it.
for the first in
our relationship when i left
my girlfriend that night
i kissed
her with judas lips.

Falling for petals

The Stranger

she gifted me a smile
in passing and it did
something to me
that i cannot truly explain.

it did something to me
that kept me revisiting
it in my mind
again and again.

i didn't know her name
or what was on her mind,

i might never see her again,
but the smile she left
with me still glows
in my mind with
the kind of brightness
that vanquish the blues away.

i saw an angel
with a smile today and
she gave that divine smile
without me asking for it.

there was a skip in her step,
diamonds in her eyes
all complementing
that unforgettable smile.
i saw a stranger today

r. A. bentinck

with a friendly smile
that was imprinted in
my mind
now as i think about her
all i can do is smile.

thank you stranger
with a friendly smile.

Falling for petals

Tales

your eyes tell
a thousand tales and
i have already taken
a seat under a shaded tree,
let them speak to me.

your eyes beckon me
to come closer,
tell me about
your concealed fantasies,
tell me about
your late-night yearnings.

reveal to me you most
treasures secrets.
your batting eyes
they appeal to me.

tell me about your goals and dreams,
tell me about all the things
you want to accomplish,
all the things you want to change
in this world,

tell me about those obstacles
and stumbling blocks
that stand in your way.

tell me about you.

r. A. bentinck

<u>Butterfly Wisdom</u>

butterflies don't go
racing after flowers,
with instinctive timing
and awareness
they find the most suitable
flower to seek rest
and refreshing nectar nutrients.

you can never catch
the ideal butterfly by
chasing it down.

they say you sit and wait.

you soak in their frolicking flights,
you enjoy their delicate balancing acts
on supple petals,
you cherish their plethora of colours
and their aerial majesty.

butterflies don't go
dashing after roses
they are attracted by
the healthiest and
the most suitable ones,
then bask in the liquid glory.

you will never savour
the inherent beauty
of a butterfly by racing after it

Falling for petals

in fields and gardens.

you sit and wait,
wait,
wait,
and wait patiently
then the butterfly
will find you,

it will sync with you,
it will become you and
only then can you truly
enjoy and appreciate
the magic of a butterfly.

r. A. bentinck

Un-See

i saw you today
and now i cannot
unsee you.

you sauntered into the halls
of my welcoming mind
now i can't get rid of you.

what did you do to me?

i am remembering
your comforting countenance
that set my uncertain mind at ease
and give my thoughts wings.

i saw your flashlight smile today
and now i cannot
unsee you.

you have taken a permanent seat
at my creative table
and you are now dining
with my wildest writing fantasies.

i saw your sweet face today
and now i cannot
unsee you.

i heard your tantalising whispers,
digested your every word,

Falling for petals

heard the sincerity in your declarations
and felt the passion in everything
you said.
i fell for your uniqueness today
and now i cannot
unsee you.

r. A. bentinck

Her World

i never knew how
easily this visible world could
dissolved into nothingness
until i spent a moment
in her world.

i gazed keenly into the depths
of her engaging eyes
and a whole new world
appeared incrementally,

i got captivated by
her dimpled smiles
and caught up
in a world of sweet possibilities,
i felt her buttery skin
and suddenly
an unfamiliar and exciting rhythm
dominated the left side
of my chest.

she giggled and laughed
and the music she made
took me away
to soothing places
where i tasted and felt
sweet reverie.

she spoke with such
intellectual fluency and

Falling for petals

i was bedazzled by
her wittiness,
her analytical prowess,
her insightfulness,
her wealth
of extensive knowledge and
mind absorbing conversation.

i got a whiff
of her natural bouquet
and i had to swiftly bridle
my galloping imagination
and out-of-control emotions.

until today,
i never knew how easy
it was for this complex
and sometimes confusing world
to fade away until
i spent some time
in her world.

r. A. bentinck

Longer Next Time

she kissed me
like the morning sun
and
my days became
brighter and warmer.
so i asked her politely,
can you make it
longer next time?

we got engrossed
in an intellectual conversation
but time and
our respective responsibilities
forced us to leave in
the middle of it all.

so i told her
we need to make it happen
longer next time.

once in my dreams, i kissed
her sugary lips
but in the heat of the dream
i got a wake-up call
from my roommate.

so with frustration,
i informed him
to let me sleep
longer next time.

Falling for petals

she embraced me
as she said goodbye
and i had to interrupt
her departure by asking her,
can you make it
last a bit
longer next time?

there is something about her
that makes me feel like
i can never get enough of her.

despite how much time
we spend together and
how much we enjoy
each other's company,

when it comes time to leave
i always feel the need
to tell her,
we need to do this
longer next time.

r. A. bentinck

<u>Falling for Petals</u>

nothing prepares you
for the experiences;
not the advice of your parents,
the shit-talking from your boys.
nothing prepares you
for the softness
of the touching and touches
of petals in your hands.
so here i am
falling for petals.

i have learned that
some petals are addictive.
the softness makes me weak.
i felt for a petal yesterday,
i am falling for another petal today
and somehow i know
i will fall for another petal
again tomorrow.

so here i am
standing here trying
to make sense of it all
as i am falling for petals.

nothing prepares you
for the experiences;
the words of the sweet talkers
never reveal the underlying
issues you will face.

Falling for petals

the game of the players
never prepares you for
being played.

you get lost in the fragrance,
captivated by the sweetness
and hypnotise by the
never-ending seductiveness.
so here i am
falling for petals again.

r. A. bentinck

Are you Really Ready?

slow down rookie
don't get so excited and
carried away by
her physical grandeur.

she comes with more than
a pretty face,

she comes with more than
a big booty,

she comes with more than
a glowing smile,

she comes with more than
a coca-cola bottle shape.
slow down brother.

hidden beneath all of her
ideal physical attributes
is a bouquet of heartbreak,

a plethora of grief,
a history shattered trust,
a bevy of abuse,
and fear of trusting and
loving again.

are you ready to deal
with all of that?

Falling for petals

are you really prepared
to deal with it?

are you equipped to navigate
her complex terrain?
because it's not if
but when it will one day seep
to the surface.

and then you will struggle
to see her beauty
amidst the dominance of all
she is carrying beneath the surface.

she is more than a pretty face
and a beautiful body
she is a woman with a history
of scars and broken.

are you really ready
to deal with it all?
are you?

slow down my friend,
don't get so excited and
carried away by
her physical grandeur,

look a little deeper,
be more attentive,
listen to her attentively.
there is so much more

to her than her natural riches.
what are you going to do
when you find yourself sitting and
crying for her pains?

what are you going to do
when you catch yourself sitting
and crying her tears?

what are you going to do
when her anger gets
the best of her on those
unexpected days
then she changes into Cruella de Vil
and you are now just another
one of the one hundred
and one dalmatian?

what are you going to do
when grief and pass memories
disfigures her pretty face and
robbed her of her composure
and sweetness?
what are you going to do
when she surrenders to sadness
and refuses to talk to you?

refuses to take your calls,
refuses to see you,
looks at you like you are
the worst thing on the face
of the earth.

Falling for petals

what are you going to do then?

are you really ready to deal
with all of her?
are you?

slow down brethren,
don't trip all over
her breathtaking beauty
and silky charm,
she comes with concealed scars,
inflicted by insensitive fools
who never saw beyond
her physical wealth.
calm down my brethren,
take a long slow deep breath
and after reading all of this
ask yourself honestly.

am i really ready to deal
with all of her?
are you?

r. A. bentinck

<u>Confused</u>

she came like a thief
on a moonless night and took
everything i possessed.

she gently stole my innocence,
robbed me of my timidity,
stripped me of my cultivated pride,
unlocked the steel vault to
my hidden fantasies
and intentionally exposed
the freak in me.

she came like a skilled thief
and caught me by surprise
and she took almost everything
now i am left
breathless,
senseless,
and
distressed,
because she left with
all my fledgling hopes
and blossoming dreams.

what a woman.
what an experience.
what unintentional destruction
she has left in her stiletto path.

she came like a veteran thief

Falling for petals

on a moonless night and took
everything i had.

r. A. bentinck

Her Exceptional Smiles (for Shakkeene)

effortless perfection, that's how
i would describe her smiling.

it wouldn't be an exaggeration
for me to conclude that
she was fairy dust sprinkled
with the rarest collection of smiles.

she possesses smiles
that reflects an assortment
of the best smiles
from the ancestors of yore.

her smiles are extraordinary
in so many ways.
her pleasant smile will
tease you,
her gentle smile will
please you.

her radiant smile will
mesmerise you,
her charming smile will
seduce you,

her satisfied smile will
bring you joy,
her scintillating smile will
hypnotise you,

Falling for petals

her carefree smile will
liberate you from bleak places,
and
her humorous smile will
frolic with
your unbridled imagination
in inconceivable ways.

this is not equity.

no one woman should possess
such a glistening array
of mind-altering smiles.

r. A. bentinck

Beyond Physical Beauty

she once asked me,
"how do you see me?"
this is how i would describe her
to the world:

she is not
your regular cookie-cutter beauty,
our world has
a surplus of those types.

she is a rarity.

she will entice you with her
blinding physical beauty
then floor you with
her unexpected intellectual brilliance.
she is more than beautiful.

she can engage you
on a sophisticated level
that leaves you yearning for
self-improvement afterward.

she is intellectual.

she has that rare combination
of beauty, brain,
and elegant confidence
that is infectious on so many levels.
she is all woman.

Falling for petals

she is beyond beauty,
she a specimen
of the 'ideal woman.'

COVID-19 (Lover's Blues)

two weeks of quarantine?!
what the hell!

babe, how am i suppose
to survive without you
by my side?

this is going to be torture.

we will facetime.

that's not the same as
lying in your arms
while i get lost in your eyes.

i will call you every day.
that's not the same as
sitting in your company
while i get hypnotise by
your natural pheromones.

two weeks of quarantine?

this is frigging ridiculous!
damn you coronavirus,
damn you!

how the hell am i suppose
to make it without my baby
by my side?

Falling for petals

how?

somebody better find a cure quick
because i am not going just sit here
talking to a screen all the time.

two weeks of quarantine?

this is blasted preposterous!
damn you coronavirus,
damn you!

babe, clam down,
before you know it
these two weeks will be over.

i rather have a healthy you
in two weeks than a sick one
just because you won't wait this out.

i hate it when her level headed
and logical reasoning is correct.

Just Like

just like fresh coconut oil
on my dry skin,
you add soothing smoothness
and glow to my life.

just like my favourite cologne,
Calvin Klein's obsession,
you add a sweet and
intoxicating fragrance
to my everyday existence.

just like the flowers outside
my morning window
you add colour, aroma,
and elegance to my life

and for that i am grateful.
just like the evening birds
at innocent play,
you add sweet songs
to my life
and
my days are
no longer dreary.

like my favourite blanket
on rainy days
you add pleasant warmth
and comfort
to my chilly moments.

Falling for petals

in so many ways
you add life and light
to my days.

r. A. bentinck

Sinned

father forgive me.
one look at her and
i swear i have already
sinned a thousand times.

forgive me.
one look at her and
my mind
went to dirty places in a jiffy,

my imagination
has gone viral,
and my loin
is overreacting.

right now i am assessing possibilities
of being with her.
i wasn't prepared for this
believe me, people
i wasn't.

father, please forgive me.
she passed by me and
i couldn't recuse myself
from the herd
of animalistic emotions.

i wasn't ready for any of it,
i swear i wasn't ready.
father, i beg of you,

Falling for petals

forgive me, please.

i didn't know one look at her
would have caused me
to sin a thousand times
in my mind.
damn, she is fine!

r. A. bentinck

<u>Unprepared</u>

nothing prepares you
for the moment
your breath is stolen
from right under your nose.

you can never how strong
you are until you get
too weak to resist
the temptation that is
breathing on your neck.

her dainty words and
exotic fragrance caress
your senses forcing you
to ask for permission to breathe.
the flirtatious thoughts
that now populate
your disciplined mind
seems to take on a life of their own.

the raging blood in your veins,
the out of control emotions,
it's getting too heavy to carry.

she seems to come out
from nowhere and took
all my self-discipline
into custody.

Falling for petals

That Smile

that smile.
i have seen your smile
so many times, before
and somehow
i am yet to find
the right combination
of words
to truly describe
what i see.

your smile.
i have felt it
so many times before
but every time
i see it
i feel like
i am feeling it
for the first time.

the look in your eyes
when you smile,
the glow on your face
that it paints,
and the beauty
of it all
makes each moment
in your smile
priceless.

r. A. bentinck

On the Dance Floor

she is courteous
and respectful in person.

the sweetest and most
charming personalities
to be around.

but when she gets
on the dance floor
she instantly mutates into
a sultry goddess.

her once petite
and decent waistline
becomes a gyrating and
grinding machine.
her rhythmic moves are flawless
and she drops dance moves
that makes your mouth water
and your loins boil
with fierce desires.

her expanding waistline speaks
a dance language that simple
to interpret but difficult
to erase from the overactive mind.

she is a lady in daily life
but on the dance floor
she is a tantalising sensation

Falling for petals

that leaves you weak
in the knees and
drenched with perspiration.

r. A. bentinck

Morality

i am flabbergasted
by her natural beauty.
she seems flawless.

an empress
in a mini body fitted dress.
a temptress
at her seductive best.

while my imagination
was taking flight
and sensual faculties
was throwing a tantrum
my morality stepped in.

it calmly reminded
that i have a queen at home,
who has been by my side
through
the good,
the bad
and indifferent.

morality reminded me
that not all that glitter
is pure gold
and some fancy wrapped gifts
aren't worth unwrapping.
i am not going to lie,
she is a rare specimen

Falling for petals

of a goddess with
true natural beauty.
but at this point in my journey
i cannot take my eyes off
the ultimate prize.

i bridled my natural
temptation instincts and
i coaxed by sensual faculties,
reminding them
that we have lots of sweetness
at home waiting for us.

r. A. bentinck

Window Connections

the curtain in
her opened window
flirted with
the soft morning breeze
on this rousing day,

and her dazzling smile
greeted me enthusiastically.

in a strange way
despite seeing her
for the first time
it felt like we knew
each other for an eternity.

the nearby butterflies
danced merrily
to the gentle sound
of her cheerful voice
as she greeted me
with a pleasant good morning.

something
about her countenance
penetrated me to my core
in an uplifting way.

and my fast-paced steps
slowed automatically
just enough

Falling for petals

for me to catch
and
bottle every ounce
of her pleasantries.
as i continued my journey
something muttered
to my inner being,
you need to pass
this way again.

No Sweet Talkin'

i don't come bearing
sugary words
coated in
honey flavoured flattery.

i come clothed
with simplicity.

i was raised
by a mother
who taught me
how to love
and respect women.

she did it with
the unconscious examples
she quietly set.
i don't always ware
the flashy clothes
and drive the latest bima
but i know
your value
and your worth.

i am here
because i recognise
the woman and
queen in you.
i see more than
your flawless beauty,

Falling for petals

i have picked up
on your intellectuality
and that's sexy to me.
i don't come
with a hidden agenda
i am here to celebrate
and take all of you in.

r. A. bentinck

Falling for petals

Developing interest
Sowing Seeds of Connection

"Each day my love grows deeper, deeper than I never thought before."
-Unknown

r. A. bentinck

Hooked

she sauntered by in
a tight-fitting black dress
and promptly arrested
my attention without warning,
my eager eyes instantly became
a focused laser beam
as i carefully track her every step.

my heartbeat quickly synced
with each click
her stiletto heels made
on the well-polished floor.

in a room full of eligible guys
her searching gaze
found my roaming eyes.
now we a caught up
in an erotic dance
of uncertain emotions
and adventurous yearnings.

in a crowded room
full of fine guys,
her angelic eyes found mine,
now we are lost in a fantasy
of romantic possibilities
and what could be before
this lovely night is over.

r. A. bentinck

<u>When Again</u>

when do i see you again?
when do i get to bask in
the glorious glow
of your serene smile?

when do i get to hear
the rhythmic rhythms
of your heart
again?

when do i see you again?

when do i get to see those
dimpled smiles again?
when do i get to sit
in the luxurious comfort of
your motivating company
again?

when can i see you again?

when do i get the opportunity
to get lost in your fascinating eyes?
when do i get to revel in
your welcoming embrace?
when can i feel your tender hands
again?

when do i get the chance
to be with you again?

Falling for petals

its only been weeks
since i last saw you,
but it feels like ages.

when do i see you again?

r. A. bentinck

__Fugacious__

there was something in that
scrumptious but fleeting moment.
there was something ethereal
and eternal about you.

you wore your tease
with such elegant ease
now it's etched
in the annals of my mind.

there was something fluid about
the way glided across
the parched earth
while whistling birds
sang songs of praise to you.
you carried your temptation
with such innocent confidence
now i have a carousel
of your sweetness
while trapped in a cocoon
of what-ifs.

there was something
entrancing about you today.
something in your blinding smile
and that glow in your girlish eyes
that has me in a lust-filled daze
long after you departed.

Falling for petals

Stars

i am relaxing under
a blanket of stars
in the cool of the evening
while thoughts
of you romances
my fertile mind.

i am laying here going wild
with anticipation.

somehow tonight
my restless mind
can't seem to get enough
of you.
so here i am roaming
the endless fields of your
unconquered sensuality.
i am laying here sorting through
images of your unending beauty.

this evening i have
given into the feelings
of your insatiable temptations,
i have decided to let my
imagination gallop carefree
in the pastures of your sweetness.

r. A. bentinck

<u>Her World</u>

i never knew how
easily this visible world could
dissolved into nothingness
until i spent a moment
in her world.

i gazed keenly into the depths
of her engaging eyes
and a whole new world
appeared incrementally,

i got captivated by
her dimpled smiles
and caught up
in a world of sweet possibilities,
i felt her buttery skin
and suddenly
an unfamiliar and exciting rhythm
dominated the left side
of my chest.

she giggled and laughed
and the music she made
took me away
to soothing places
where i tasted and felt
sweet revery.

she spoke with such
intellectual fluency and

Falling for petals

i was bedazzled by
her wittiness,
her analytical prowess,
her insightfulness,
her wealth
of extensive knowledge and
mind absorbing conversation.

i got a whiff
of her natural bouquet
and i had to swiftly bridle
my galloping imagination
and out-of-control emotions.

until today,
i never knew how easy
it was for this complex
and sometimes confusing world
to fade away until
i spent some time
in her world.

r. A. bentinck

Braveheart

i always wanted *you,*
from the first time i laid
eyes on you,
i felt the need to be with you.
she said, with a coy smile
and wicked eyes.

from behind confident eyes
and with lips so soft
they eased there way
into the depth of my
strong morals.

for months i watched
from a distance
with wet desires
and an overactive imagination
i always wanted you.

her hands held me tenderly
and her seductive natural fragrance
commanded my pores
and the hairs on my body
to stand tall and proud.

i have been doing things
to you in my mind
for a very long time
and i always hoped
this day will come.

Falling for petals

*now here we are and
i am willing and ready
to show you all the things i have been
doing with you in my mind.*

r. A. bentinck

<u>Body Heat</u>

i lay in the bosom
of the darkness of this evening,
i am cold and shivering
my blanket is useless,
my mind is skipping
in between your enticing memories.

this is not right.
me being here all alone
with your memories
toying with my explosive desires.

it's not right, baby.

i need you here with me,
i need your body heat,
i need you to please me,
i promise i wouldn't
do anything you don't
want me to.

come on over baby.

i wanna feel your body heat,
i want you to rock me to sleep,
i want you to whisper
those smooth words in my ears,
i wanna lay right in the richness
of all your tenderness.
i should not be here

Falling for petals

all alone,
you should be here baby.
i know it will feel good
when we let loose.
i know it would.
come on baby, please
come over tonight.

r. A. bentinck

Troubled Soul

what do you do
when her friendly face
mutates with grief?

what do you do
when you suddenly get
the blame for things
that you didn't do?

her once excited voice
has become a dagger
to the heart of your happiness.

her joy-filled laughter
fades into nothingness
and you no longer
recognize the person
she has become.
you cannot relate to
this unrecognized being.

how do you speak
the language of happiness
to her stubborn and
persistent sadness?

how do you find
the solutions to
her sudden misery?
how do you comfort

Falling for petals

and console her burdened soul?
how to you comprehend it all?
often she becomes
the host of a foreign entity
that i cannot recognize,
she is no longer
the woman i use to know,

she seems like an alien being.
i don't recognize this woman
in my life at this time.

her once supple body
has become frigid by
her depressing thoughts,

her brilliant smile has been
extinguished by the waters
of her toxic reservoir.
where did she go?
what can i do
to guide her back
to where she belongs?

r. A. bentinck

Turn Me Over

sometimes it's good
to surrender,
give up the need
to be in control
just go with the flow.

my position of dominance
was not cutting it anymore
so she turned me over
in one clean and swift motion.

she introduced me
to motions
i have never seen or
experienced before.

but i willingly let myself
go with the flow
of the moment.

that flow caused sensations
that left me
gasping,
clawing,
twitching,
yearning,
and singing to
satisfactory heaven.

she turned me over

Falling for petals

and taught me a lesson
in the sweetness of uncertainty.

r. A. bentinck

Manhattan Bound

leaving brooklyn on
a manhattan bound train,
in the heart of rush hour
with standing seats only
but fortunately, i have you
close to me.

we quickly settled into
our little world
amidst this sardine-crammed
environment.

holding on tight jostling
to secure our prize space
as we brace ourselves for
the long ride.
despite the crowded space
you were still the center
of my world.

i was still able to hear your
sweet words amidst
the noise of the train wheels
kissing the tracks
at top speed.

i felt the warmth of your breath in
the freezer like setting.
my senses were heightened
and i slowly sip your

Falling for petals

smooth fragrance
to my heart's content,
our bodies gradually
develops a familiar heat
and i snuggle you
a little closer in
the scarcity of space.

our eyes locked in
an engaging conversation
and your endless smile
somehow makes this journey
tolerable.

in a sea of foreign faces
and metallic sounds
you close to me
was the best place to be
on this manhattan bound train.

r. A. bentinck

The Guilt Complex

she kissed me and the purest
of love flowed from her lips,
and immediately i knew
i would never be able
to return that unconditional love
she gave so effortlessly.

then for the first time
guiltiness introduced itself to me.

we sat under the welcoming shade
of a blooming tree and
she told me her untold stories
because she said
her spirit trusted me.

silently i started having
a conversation with guilt
just because i questioned
my ability to carry the burdens
of her trust.

she looks at me with so much
assuredness,
she believes in me even when
i don't believe in myself,
she trusts me with her life
and her love and this
makes me feel guilty.
she supports me in ways

Falling for petals

i am yet to truly fathom.
i often ask myself
i am deserving of her
and then silently retreated
to my guilty room.

r. A. bentinck

Comfort

like a well made bed
at the end of a long
and arduous day,

like freshly blended
cherry juice
with my morning breakfast,

like the reassuring words
of a loving mother
on your first day of school,

like the welcoming smile
of your lovers standing by
the open door to greet you,
like the sound of your
favourite song on
those lonely days,

like the sound of the sea
as it kisses the sand
on the seashore,

she means so many things
to me in so many ways.

Falling for petals

Turn Me Over

sometimes it's good
to surrender,
give up the need
to be in control
just go with the flow.

my position of dominance
was not cutting it anymore
so she turned me over
in one clean and swift motion.

she introduced me
to motions
i have never seen or
experienced before.
but i willingly let myself
go with the flow
of the moment.

that flow caused sensations
that left me
gasping,
clawing,
twitching,
yearning,
and singing to
satisfactory heaven.

she turned me over
and taught me a lesson

r. A. bentinck

in the sweetness of uncertainty
and letting go to live
in the flow.

Falling for petals

<u>You</u>

on those days when it gets
too much to take
i know i can count
on you.

when no one else
understands my fluctuating moods
you do,

when the world gets so harsh
that i bleed tears
you are always there
to heal my aching wounds.

it's such a wonderful feeling
just thinking
about you
 knowing that you are
in my life.

you add so much essence
to this life and heart of mine
i just want to take this moment
to say
thank you,
just for being you
and tolerating me
in so many ways.

r. A. bentinck

__Rhythms of the Night__

my pores surfaced
about the flood of perspiration,
the hair on my skin
is submerged in this
warm slippery river.

in the still of the night
two hearts sync with a mutual beat
and the dominating sounds
are sounds of sensual satisfaction.

the varying pitch and tones
create a melodic symphony
that's beautiful to the learned ear.

two bodies in unison obeying
the unseen instructions
from the inconspicuous
musical conductor.

my pores get submerge
by the deluge of perspiration,
and the hair on my skin
struggle to stay upright
as they battle the constant flow
of the now warm salty water.

When I Say I Love You

when i say i love you
i am not talking about
the cookie-cutter kinda love,

when i say i love you
it means i will walk
with you on those
arduous days when
your feet hurt and
everything pains
in an uncomfortable way.

when i say i love you
i am not talking about
the kinda love that lust
off of your body,
i am talking about
a love that appreciates you,
body and soul,
where i take the time
to worship you and
your spirituality.

when i say i love you
it's not the selfish kinda love,
it's the kind of love
that allows me to know
when to shut up and
listen to you even when
i want to speak,

r. A. bentinck

it's the kinda love
that allows me to sit
with you in your silence
as we listen to the
wisdom of
the whispering wind.

it's that kinda love.
when i say i love you
it means on cold evenings
when it gets extremely frigid
i will give you
the t-shirt off my back,

i will give you the warmth
of my skin and
i will embrace you
so close that
the chilly breeze will be
left out in the cold.

when i say i love you
i am not talking about
the cookie-cutter kinda love,

it's love on a deeper level,
love on a deeper vibration,
a love that
will fight with you,
a love that
will fight for you
against your psychological demons,

Falling for petals

against your forgettable past,

a love that will love you
beyond and despite
your faults and scars,

a love that will cherish you
just because you are you.

Transformational

you came, you saw,
you healed.

seems like you came
from out of nowhere
and
you made my life better.

you came, you saw,
relived.

you made my smile
wider,
you soothed the pains
in my breaking heart
and
you lit up the dark areas
of my dull life.

you came, you saw,
you teach.

i didn't ask for it
but
you gave me
good love.
i didn't recognise it
immediately
but you made me
wiser.

Falling for petals

you came, you saw,
you loved.

when i was cold
you kept me warm.
when i was weak
you were my strength.
when i couldn't speak
you were my voice.
when i was hungry
you fed me.

you came, you saw,
you transformed me
into a better man.

r. A. bentinck

Wishful Thinking

i want so badly
to stop the hands of time.

we both know
its gonna fly now that
we are together.

hold me close.
let me take in
all of your fragrance.
let's melt into one.

how quickly we forget
time and place when
our hearts speak as one.

let's find a way to stop
time from passing by.

here we are
once again
playing those hiding games,
sheltering our feelings
under false disguises.

every touch you give
to me feels so divine.

every word you speak
takes on a seductive meaning.

Falling for petals

i just want to run away
with you in a timeless existence.
something about being
with you feels so sublime.
i want to create a world
where we can strip naked
and bare all our feelings
for each other
unashamedly.

r. A. bentinck

Will You?

will you be there
with me
when i have
to walk in my pouring rain?

will you be there
for me
when my burdens get
too much to carry?

will you be there
to lead me
when my tears blind my sight?

will you be by my side
when my confused emotions
cloud my better judgment?

i come from a place
of hurting too
and sometimes i do get weak.

on those days
can i count on you
to be there for me?

can i count on you
to be there with me?

Falling for petals

Mary Jane

the smoke gradually
escaped through
the opening of her savoury lips
as she eased slowly
toward me with
begging lips.

she craved my affection
so she blessed me
with one of her
tantalizing kisses.

it made me high.
her mood was mellow,
her tongue did a lot more
investigating this time around
as it roamed the walls
of my mouth.

her saliva was like
honey to my parched appetite
and her comforting embrace
revealed a unique blend
of her favourite perfume
mixed with Mary Jane.

she intensified the romanticism
of the moment
by gently blowing the smoke
she so carefully reserved

for me behind sealed lips.

it was deliciously erotic.

her smoked flavoured lips
left me in a trance.

we suspended words
for a moment
and
our eyes locked
in a gaze that spoke
of the true feelings
swirling around
in the smoke-filled air.

Falling for petals

Maintaining Interest
Long Term Commitment

"Falling in love is easy. Falling in love with the same person repeatedly is extraordinary."
-Crystal Woods

r. A. bentinck

Falling for petals

Running on Broken Glass

it erupted one day:
the rage
the temper
the tantrum
and
the uncontrolled anger.

now i am living in fear
fixing a shattered car window,
sleeping with one eye open
and living in an uneasy street.

turns out i was living with
a gorgeous woman
who also had a riddled soul
and fragile emotions.
what am i to do now?
my peace of mind
is now a stranger to me,
and i cannot deal with
the fears that come from
her now unpredictable personality.

this is all treacherous and
unsettling to me.

r. A. bentinck

Transformation

he is now... face to face
with a woman who he doesn't
recognise anymore.

her once-loving eyes
are now glazed with
hate and anger.

her gentle and soothing voice
is now high pitched and
filled with rage.

he stands there and his
now heightened attention
switches between her unrecognisable eyes
and the screwdriver in a vice-like lock
in her shivering hands.

this is not the affectionate woman
he grew to love over the years
this cannot be the same woman.

what triggered this behaviour?
what flipped her switch?

he stood there battling
his instinctive macho demeanour
to stand and fight it out
while grappling with

Falling for petals

his fearful thoughts and
the constant her to run.

what triggered this sudden change?
what did he do?
the situation is too intense
for him to think straight
and clear.

r. A. bentinck

Relentless

it's not the fact that
i don't recognize that
i would have erred
in the past.

i am no saint and
i don't claim to be,

but her ability to remember
and recall every detail
from past wrongdoings
stabs me in hurtful ways.
my psychological
and mental health
is under a barrage of nagging.
one innocent act
a slip of the mouth and
it all goes up in flames.

my peace-filled present
can swiftly take wings
under the machine gun like
hurling of accusation stones.

she can be unrelenting
and insensitive at times
with her recollecting and
over analysing
of my past behaviours
and past shortcomings.

Hardship (Broken Petals)

she was planted
in uncertain gardens
and watered with with
fear and molestation.

she bloomed in an environment
with paltry nutrients
and rationed love.

now she is allergic to
all that is good.

she wanna repeat
the sad stories
over and over again,
she wants to relive
the painful memories
over and over again,

she hates the sweet sounds
of whispering love
and
rejects tender touches
and gentle kisses.

she has grown accustomed
to the hurtings.

she seems to want more
of the hurt,

she seems to want more
of the pain,
she wants to tell
more sad stories.
how do i go on
loving her through
all her pains?

how do you love
a broken flower
without being affected
by her hurting petals?

how do you love her
beyond her beyond
and out of her grief?

Falling for petals

The Holy Ones

while their parents and friends
had the hands outstretched
to the lord in prayers
and talking in tongues,
seeking deliverance
for their sinning souls,

he had her up against
the wall of pleasure
making stranges yet
familiar sounds.

while her nosy neighbours were
busy looking out for her
and checking the time,
she was too preoccupied
counting how many times
he took her to cloud nine
to be bothered.

while his friends were
excited about getting tickets
to the ball game
he was caught up with
finding a clever scheme
to secretly slip away with her
unnoticed.
in society's eyes,
it was elicit,
it was wrong,

r. A. bentinck

it was ungodly,
it was immoral
and downright
stupid...
somewhere in the backs
of their indoctrinated and
traditional thinking minds
it felt wrong too
but
it felt so damn good
and they could care less.

this wasn't made up feelings,
it was mutual respect
and attraction,
they connected on
a deeper level,
existed on a higher vibration

and they surrendered
to the calls of the wild
and dangerous side.
so while their loved ones
were praying and

the faultless were busy
judging them
they were too caught up
with the natural feelings
of the moment to be
distracted.
they were too occupied

Falling for petals

savouring
the essence of each divine moment
that took their breaths away,
made their knees rattled,
generated beads
of glorious perspirations
and a plethora of unforgettable
memories.

r. A. bentinck

Broken

beautiful girls don't often
come complete and
unblemished.

sometimes they come broken
and with missing pieces.
scared memories,
with cracked heart and
tattered emotions.

beauty is not a guaranteed
sign of wholeness.

beauty is not a certainty
of emotional stability,
her natural beauty only speaks
of who and what she is
on the surface.

how do you deal with this?
how do you cope with it?
how do you help with healing?
how are you suppose navigate
those difficult moments?

some women are skilled
at concealing
their emotional cracks,
and this often catches you
by surprise when you

Falling for petals

eventually, get to see
how many cracks exist
and how deep those cracks run.

r. A. bentinck

Not Again!

i was frozen from disbelief
after i heard the familiar words
falling from an unfamiliar mouth
yet again.

in her eyes was
the kind of pain
you couldn't stare into
for too long,

and after her courage wilted
under the pressures
of her painful past,
the tears leaked from
her now
heavy eyelids.
and i find myself repeating
a refrain i know too well,
not again?
not again!
not this.
not this again.

the stories:
my dad molested me,
so did my brothers,
my uncle and
the next-door neighbour.
now my husband is virtually
doing the same to me.

Falling for petals

now as i recollect
the frequent and unexplained
mood swings and
the fragile trust

it all starts to make more sense now,
she was abused.
i am blessed with a gem
who was tarnished by some
of the very males who was
supposed to protect her.

now my task of loving her
has been made even more difficult
through no flaut of mine.

i have heard this story
so many times before
and as a listener to it again,
it never gets easier for me
to hear.

r. A. bentinck

Cooking for You

my cooking for you
is like writing about you.

the flavours cause
my taste buds to erupt
with excited appreciation.

i skillful blend
of herbs and spices
to enhance
the tantalising aromas
that heightens my senses.

my cooking for you
it is like writing about you.

you force me to bring
my best to the process
because anything else will
be unacceptable.

the wide array of colour
is a feast for the eyes
as i devour the satisfying
combinations of diverse hues.

my cooking for you
is like writing about you.
savour and enjoy
every drop of spicy flavours.

Falling for petals

Circumstantial scars

"how did fingernail marks
get on your back
in multiple places?"

it's one of the most
frightening question
you can hear from someone
who means so much to you.

it's often one of the most
heart racing accidental discoveries
you don't want to be
a part of it.

now all the unexplained
late nights start to take
on new meaning,

all the unanswered questions
starts to take on a life
of there own,

all the suspicious looks
and unexplained silence
starts to add up.

how do you explain
those scars away?
now all the possible answers
that pop in your head

r. A. bentinck

don't make any sense and
not even your new-found
silence can explain them away.
"how did you get
these fingernails marks
on your back?"

you freeze in silent thought
as you search for an answer
that hopefully makes sense.

how do you answer that question
without hurting someone?
how do you truly deal
with this situation?

how to you answer this question
respectfully
when the scars have answered already?

Falling for petals

Poison Ivy

a saint i am not
and i never will be
but it's the things she
does to me even though
i have been nothing but good to her.

i have gone out of my way
to make her feel safe,
to listen to her troubles
and concerns,
to strive to make her laugh
and smile in genuine ways
but

covertly she has been plotting
my destruction.
saved private messages
and photos that show too much
is dangled in front of my nose
with promissory threats
to share them on the internet.

she surreptitiously records our conversations
and ask the most vulnerable questions
not intending to heal
but to wound me in my tender places.

she can go days without responding
to my calls and messages
even though she knows

r. A. bentinck

i am worried sick about
her welfare and wellbeing.

she is hell bend on playing games
with my heart while
all i do is take care of hers.
what type of woman is she?
isn't she poison ivy?

Falling for petals

Difficult Days

don't be fooled
by the honeymoon period.
difficult days are ahead,
lots of them.

it's not if, but a when.
they all have a story
of betrayal and unforgettable pains.

the real question is,
are you equipped to deal
with those days?
can you negotiate the perilous terrain?

the painful stories,
the mood swings,
the fears?
the remembering,
the countless uncertainties.
are you truly equipped
to deal with it all?

i have a long time ago
lost of the stories
of abuse,
betrayal and,
fractured trust.

i am also experienced enough
to know that scares can only

be hidden for so long,

when your love ones
find comfort and trust in you
they will open up,
they will tell you
the untold stories,
they will share the pains,
the broken bits,
the sordid past,
and it can overwhelm you.

it will hurt you,
disturb your balance
and peace of mind.
they will force you
to face and ask complex questions
with no immediate and
logical answers.

are you battle trained
for those difficult days ahead?
will you still be there?
will you still provide a shoulder
for tears to rest?

will you still have a nonjudgmental ear
for the painful recollecting
of past stories?
will the ' i love you'
that you shared
survive it all?

Falling for petals

will you still feel the love?
will you still give love
unconditionally?

are you man enough
to stand by and with her
through those difficult days?

r. A. bentinck

Silent Conversations

it's not the
arguments and disagreements
that gets to you often,

its the conversations you
have with yourself
during the quiet moments
that messes with your mind.

that's when you start
to see the magnitude
and the stupidity
in the things,
you would have said
and done.
that when you start to see
how big you have
fucked up
and how much
damage
you have done and caused.

that when you start to see
you have reached
the point of no return.

and often you ask
the question why?

Falling for petals

A Place of Hurt

her words:
it's not that i don't
love you, baby
but i come from a place of hurt,
its what i have come
to know as normal
for as long as I can remember.
and you loving me
so unconditionally
really feel weird,
i am not accustomed to this.

it feels faked.
it's like i am waiting for
the abuse to start any day now,
i am waiting for the disrespect to flow,
it always comes, always.

try to understand,
please, baby.
i am coming from a place
that hurt.
this is all new to me.

when you touch me
its not that i don't like it,
its not that your touches aren't
gentle
is just that the sometimes
they trigger unwanted memories,

memories of me being hurt,
memories that never seem to fade-
i am sorry, baby.
please be patient with me
i have come a long way
and i still have a long way to go.
i don't want to be hurt again,
i don't want to feel those pains
ever again.

just walk with me,
talk with me,
listen to me,
hold me,
hold me, baby,

i really need you now.
i really do need you.
don't ever let me go,
just reassure me that
you will be here for me.
please baby.

Falling for petals

Love's Outlaws

she is the Bonnie to my Clyde,
she will ride with me
through rapid gunfire
without batting her pretty eyes.

she is the Marcus Burnett
to my Mike Lowrey,
she always has my back,
we are Bad Boys for Life.

she is the Beyonce to my Jay Z,
got me looking so crazy right now,
her love's got me looking
so crazy right now.

they can't figure me out
they like hey is he insane
she is my young love
in A Bronx Tale,
affectionately innocent
and heartwarming.

she is the 'Syd' to my 'Dre'
in Brown Sugar,
we stumbled into romantic territory
and surrendered to the calls of love.

she is the Barbra Streisand
to my Barry Gibb,
our love will climb any mountain

near or far, and we've got nothing
to be guilty of (it oughta be illegal).

she is the Rosalie Gidharee
to my Shellie
in our Green Days by the River.

she held me in her arms
and made love to me.
she fueled my hearts' desire,
her lips caressed me
her body possessed me
now i'd keep her if i could.

she is my Carlene Davis,
Stealing Love.

Falling for petals

The Way it Was

let's go back
to taking leisure strolls
for no other reason
but to being
in each other's company.

let's go back
to finding ways
to skip the fancy restaurants
and dine under the trees
in the park.

let's go back to
slow dancing to our familiar
weakness tunes
while we lip-sync
the entire lyrics.

let's go back
to falling asleep
in each other's arm
while love ballads play
softly in the background.

let's go back
to mid-morning calls
just because we wanted
to hear each other's voices.
let's go back
to holding each other hand

on the seashore while
we frolic with
the waves and the sand.
let's go back
to the kind of love
that saw us through
all the testing times
and moments when we
thought about giving up.

let's go back
to the love that kept us
warm through all kinds of weather,

let's go back
to loving each other
beyond our flaws,
love each other
unconditionally.

Falling for petals

Complacency

he was beginning to
take her for granted.
not spending enough time
with her,
not saying the words
she always loves to hear from
his lips so,

she reminded him.
listen, when i tell you
i love you
i am not doing it
out of habit,

i am saying it to
remind you that you
are still one of the best
things to ever happen to me.

she continued
don't get complacent,
and take me for granted.
neglected love don't bloom
for long.

r. A. bentinck

Neglect

don't get complacent.
left unattended even
blooming roses will perish.
in the palms of
an irresponsible gardener
a well-manicured garden
will quickly be choked by weeds.

as they sauntered in the park
she enlightened him
with expressions of prudence
from men who would have been
where they were before.

she advised him,
bae, withered roses
don't produce nectar anymore
and the honeybees don't show up
to visit, not even to say adieu.

a rose garden in distress
will always show you clues,
you must be vigilant.

a damaged fence here,
a dry tree there,
pest-infested leaves.
there are always initial signs.
don't be complacent
you will neglect a valuable thing.

Falling for petals

Frustrated

listen, can we move on
from this place?
i want you to love me
like there will be no tomorrow.

i want you to stop
threatening me with your
unloving words
and just slay me with
your loving actions.

lay it on me,
all at once if that's possible.

just give us a chance,
let's leap with faith,
pack your baggage of fear
and ship them off to the sea.

can we move on from this
static place,
please?

i want you
to hold me
like you never held me before,

kiss me like you
never kissed me before,
make love to me like

r. A. bentinck

there will never be a tomorrow.

come on, baby.
what are you nervous about?
what is intimidating you?
what has frozen your heart?
all i ask is that you
desire me
like there is no tomorrow,
is that too much for me to ask?

Fleeting Moments

these moments with you
though few and far apart.
i count and cherish
each one of them
with all of my heart.

those moments when
we can steal away
without anyone knowing.
without anyone noticing,
i savour them all.

race and religion have dealt us
a cruel and insensitive blow.
they have us hiding
our love lights under a bushel.

they rob us of so much
of what we have in common
and is dying to share with
each other.

they have robbed us
of the burning need
to be free to love each other
the way we choose.

they are stifling our
growth together.

r. A. bentinck

as we sit here in this cosy
yet unfriendly room
i can feel the time as it slips
through our fingers
and i can feel
the cumulative sadness
coursing through our veins
transforming our faces.

it's the end of another episode,
of sneak away.
its time for us to go
our separate ways.

another kiss goodbye,
another bittersweet embrace,
another until we can find a way
to steal some more time
to be with each other.

another bouquet of memory
to be placed in the vase
of our accumulated escapades.

In My Dreams

did you feel **it?**

last night i was
butterfly caressing you.
your eyes got wide with
sensual excitement and
your skin glistened
with perspiration from
the ensuing heat.

did you feel it?

my fingers were roaming
the pastures of your
hidden fantasies and
i felt your awakened pores
speaking a familiar language
of desire.

did you hear me?

i was whispering in your ears
all the things i carried as secrets
all these years.
i have been waiting
for this opportune moment
just say what you have always
mean to me.

did you smell it?

i was wearing your favourite fragrance
the one that makes you giddy
with weakness,
that same one that breakdown
all your resistance

didn't you feel me, baby?

last night you were
in my dreams
and i didn't want
to wake up.

Unexplained Tears

if only her tears could speak
i would hear more
than what i can see
and more than she chooses
to say to me.

kept in emotions
seeping through her red and
swollen eyelids which buckle under
the weight of built-up stress
and intense pressures.

if her tears could
mirror her true hurt
and
the unspoken pains
she conceals
maybe i would
be more compassionate
in the appropriate way.

more understanding.
more sympathetic.

i have sat through
many of her unexplained tears.

i have been in the company
of tears where the only things
i was knowledgeable to offer

was my supportive shoulders
and a smattering of comforting words.

if only her tears were acid enough
to burn my skins,
maybe when they fall
from her eyes
i would be able to relate
to her on a deeper level
when she is this sad.

Falling for petals

The Ex-Factor

some girls never get over it.
there are always residues
of an ex-boyfriend
or an ex-lover loitering
in the corners of their minds.

they gossip about their ex
with friends and family
and every so often
you get compared to him,
sometimes favourably
other times unfavourably.

there are the blame games for
adverse and recurring
unsavoury behaviours.
in the ex crossfire
i am a victim of things i never created.

her apparent lack of trust
in some of my innocent actions,
her unfounded and frequent suspicions
about my precise whereabouts
and unanswered calls.

her ex-factor issues are like
the sword of Damocles
hanging over our relationship.

r. A. bentinck

The Selfish Kind

honestly, i didn't see this
in her personality
in the beginning.

is this an example
of the deception in
western courtship
that i was once warned about?

we show the best parts
of us in the beginning
and when we get
what we want
we default back
to who we truly are
at the core?
almost everything
must be done her way.

she seems to have little concern
for what i think and feel.

i am not going to lie,
she is gorgeous with
a capital g, but
her personality stinks.

she is,
to put it in simple words...
damn selfish.

Falling for petals

<u>Loving the Hurt Away</u>

they are hardest to love
when they don't know
how to love themselves.

they are harder to please
when they are never satisfied
with the love you give.

they see you through
the lens of broken trust,
scarred emotions and
a heart they no longer want.

i am a barefoot relationship soldier
in a minefield littered
with broken glass hearts.
they often put up
superficial barriers
because its what they find
safety and security in.

they are always suspicious,
always overprotecting,
always over analysing.

they come from a place
where hearts get treated
unkindly
and having a heart
is an impediment.

r. A. bentinck

it's easy to blame
but please don't;
strive
to understand
and
sympathise
you might be
there only lifeline at this time.

COVID-19 (Lover's Ecstacy)

there is no early morning alarm
blaring in our ears
while we scurry to get
ready for the day's work.

no grabbing breakfast
on the go
while we squeeze
our way through
the door trying to beat
the rush hour traffic.
trying to avoid
being late again for work.

thank you 14 days of quarantine.

we can now lay in bed
to our heart's content.
we can walk around in our
undies without worrying
about the untimely ringing
of the doorbell
by family and friends,

or having to deal with
the after blues
of coitus interruption.

we can binge-watch
our favourite television shows.

cook in our birthday suite,
pillow fight until we get tired

and watch the dirty dishes
in the sink and
turn our backs with attitude.
thank you, COVID-19
for the 14 days of quarantine.

we are going to enjoy this like
an all-expense-paid vacation
by our ungrateful employers.

we going to make every day
feels like Sunday.

we are going to convert our sofa
into a beach chair and
our rug will become the sand
on our favorite beach.

to us,
this is not a quarantine,
this is catching up on
much needed time together.
this is an occasion
to rekindle lots of old fire.

14 days
of government-imposed quarantine
with my baby by my side,
this is going to be heavenly.

Falling for petals

Just Because

just because you've never
seen me cry
doesn't mean i haven't
cried many times before.

just because you always
see me with a bright smile
doesn't mean i am not
hurting inside.

just because i choose
not to bear all my emotions
on my sleeves
doesn't mean i don't feel.

just because my heart
is not on the floor bleeding
doesn't mean
it hasn't been cut deeply.

i have walked in the valleys
of the inconsiderate
and ungrateful ones

so i have learned
to conceal and shield
my feelings and emotions.

it's not that i don't
have feelings for you,

r. A. bentinck

i haven't seen enough
of you for me to trust you
with all of what i have.

Listen to Your Woman

do you know
her true feelings for you?
do you care about those feelings?
do you know that her feelings
for you go deeper than sex?
do you truly know your woman?

do you know she sits
at night and cry
tears for you,
tears about you
and tears because of you?
do you increase her tears and fears?

did you know that
she fell for you
not because of your
material riches
but your spiritual blessings
and that deeper connection?
do you appreciate your girl?

did you know
how much she has sacrificed
just to be with you?
do you know how many
broken glass fields
she had walk through
just to get to you?
do you see the sacrifices she makes?

do you truly take time to listen
to her when she speaks
from the heart?
do you hold her so close
that she could feel the rhythm
of your heart?
does your heart beat for her?
do you listen to your lady?
*do you spend quality time with your
girlfriend?*

do you know
the unspoken pains you inflict
on heart vulnerable heart?
do you know the ways
to her tenderness?
do you cherish and nurture
her gentleness?
*can you feel the spiritual vibes of your
woman?*

you brag about knowing
what a woman wants
but do you know
the woman in your life?
do you treasure your wife?

you have broken her heart
a thousand times before
and you have left her
to walk alone in the
emotional wilderness.

Falling for petals

are you there for your lover?

do you know she trusted you
with her shattered heart?
did you know she promised
a long time ago
never to love again?
but you convinced her to change
now you are playing games
with her tender heart.
do you know how to love your woman?

do you know when she
is in pain?
can you see beneath
her sweet smile that she is hurting?
do ease or contribute
to her fears?
are you taking her for a ride?

do you know she loves
to cuddle at nights
in her sleep?
do you know what makes
her weak in the knees?
do you caress your lover often?

do you know there are times
she just needs to sit
in your company and
you don't even need to speak
for her to appreciate you deeply?

r. A. bentinck

do you give your woman
the time and the attention she deserves?

do you know there
is no easy way to break
her heart?
do you know you have
broken her heart many times before?

how do you know how to ease her pains?
take time to listen to your woman,
make time to listen to her,
spend quality time with her,
treat her like a lady,
respect her completely,
listen to your woman.
have you listened to the love of your life lately?

Falling for petals

Moments in Time

with you, i have come
to appreciate greatly
the importance of savouring
each moment in time.

one moment
we are all wrapped up
in the bosom of smiles
and joy-filled laughter
and in the wink of an eye
we are battling with
your resurfacing grotesque memories.

one moment
your eyes are bright with excitement
and your words
filled with hopeful optimism
and in a flash
the moments that follow
we find ourselves battling
to swim against
the tsunami-like waves
of hopelessness and sorrows.

these frequent fluctuating moments
are a threat to the beauty
and the life of our relationship.

as we continue to struggle
with your hurt filled daemons daily

i have gradually learned to be grateful
for the beautiful moments in time
that we shared.
i have learned to treasure,
and enjoy those elusive moments
of genuine love, and excitement,

because i can never telegraph
when it will all metaphor
for the worst
just because your memories
drags you back to a painful past.

Scented Secrets

he stepped through
the door and was greeted
by her sun-kissed smile
and love-filled personality.

he greeted her
with his signature kiss
and warm embrace.

but there was something
about him that caused her
to recoil slowly with curiosity.

he sensed it
but remained composed.
you smell different-
was the statement and question
she skillfully hurled straight
to his guilt riddled conscience
all at once.

his momentary silence was loud.

she saw the weight in his steps
and heard the cracks in the useless
words he uttered in response.

what do you mean?
...
you smell like Chanel Number 5.

...
Chanel what?

the guilt-filled chattering
in his head wiped
the smile from his face
as he walked away
wisely swallowing
the dumb ass excuses
he was about to offer
in his defence.

Falling for petals

The Cold War

tonight she was
seductively slow
and meticulous.

she made a deliberate effort
to ensure he had the best view
as she slipped into
his favourite
mouth-watering
lingerie.

she took time to put on
his favourite perfume,
the one that always brings
a flood of complements
from his hungry lips.
tonight she paid
extra attention
to the erogenous zones
he visits frequently.

she sprayed
a little extra perfume
and added extra lotion
delicate precision.

the anticipation was
unbearable.
he was boiling, throbbing,
and

salivating all at once.

she turned off the lights.
lit the scented candle.
eased into her corner
of the bed,
and curled up
with her pillow between
her legs
then gently whispered,
good night.

Falling for petals

Troubled Woman

she came from
a family tree rooted in pain
where neglect and abuse
was the liquid
that watered their roots.

she grew up in a home
where molestation,
destructive criticism,
and
fussing and fighting
was the love language
she grew to know.

now she is indifferent
to tender touches,
suspicious of genuine love,
guarded about matters
of the heart
and resentful of things romantic.

she celebrates destruction
with effortless ease
but finds it hard to see
the need for tenderness.

loving her is like
trying to make delicious bread
from stone.
being with her

is like living in a house
made of shared glass floor.
my mental health
is under constant siege,
my face is contorted with stress
and my life takes on
a new level of complexity
by the passing minutes.

i thought about leaving
so many times before
but somehow
my love for her
compels me to stay.

unhealthy?
yes, i know.

but sometimes
we must be strong enough
to love despite imperfections
and past hurt.

Falling for petals

The Cold War

tonight she was
seductively slooowwww
and meticulous.

she made a deliberate effort
to ensure he had the best view
as she slipped into
his favourite mouth-watering
lingerie.

she took time to put on
her mind-blowing
perfume combination,
the ones that always bring
a flood of complements
from his hungry lips.
tonight
she paid extra attention
to the erogenous zones
he visits frequently.

she sprayed
a little extra perfume
and added extra lotion
with delicate precision.

the anticipation was
unbearable.
the scent combination
coupled with

her irresistible curves
were creating havoc.

he was boiling,
throbbing,
and
salivating all at once.

she turned off the lights.
lit the scented candle,
and the soft light
accentuated her delicious body.

she approached his side
of the bed climbed over him
and eased into her corner
of the bed,
curled up with her pillow
between her legs
then gently whispered,
good night, baby.

Falling for petals

Seasons of Love

she came to me
in the autumn of her love.
withered and battered
because of a rough summer.

she drifting on the wings
of the northern winds.
discolored but still
true to her natural shape.

i cuddled her
throughout the harsh
and unforgiving winter,

and nurtured her
through the encouraging
and recuperating spring.
now she is in
full summer's bloom.

her radiant smile
is back,
her shimmering glow
is brilliant again,
the vitality
is back
in her every step,

the cheerful echo
in her laughter

r. A. bentinck

can be heard
from miles away
again.

it's her happy times again.

Falling for petals

Curating Memories
Reflecting and Remembering

"Love is like falling down...in the end you're left hurt, scared, and with a memory of it forever."
-Unknown

r. A. bentinck

Fa ling for petals

<u>When Memories Calls</u>

time and distance
might have to conspire
to take you away,
but our sweet memories
they never fade.

every so often they come
calling,

and i can recall those
indelible moments:
you head on my chest
while we count
the uncountable stars,

the gleam of your smile
in the dull of the night,
the reverberation
of your childish laughter
as it snaps the mute
of the night.

conditions and events
may have split us
but our unconquerable
memories survived.

i remember:
your hands in mine
while we wander

on the sands of life,
the luxury of your embrace
during my arduous days,

the inspiration of your intelligence
as you simplify
the most complex
of life's theories,
your infectious enthusiasm
and resilience.

they can take a lot away
from me
but they can't
steal or take away
our enduring memories.

when your memories
come calling
i always let them in
always.

Only Love

looking back after
all these years,
reflecting after all
we would have gone through,
now i know
it only could have been love.

looking back on all our
trials and tribulations,
our waves of laughter and tears
our joys and pains,
some were too much
for us to bear.

now i realise
it only could have been love.
when i look into her eyes,
when i see her smile,
when i am embraced by her
warm laughter,

when i lay there in her arms
and the cares of the world
just dissolve,
i have come to the realisation
it only could have been love.

the moments and events
in our lives were the thread
that wove the tapestry that is

r. A. bentinck

us today-
each colour,
each strand,
each strength,
each weakness,
each turn,
each twist,
each connection;

all a part of who and what
we are and have become.
looking back on it all
i've come to realise
it only could have been love.

and one day your time
will come
when you look back
on these experiences
that we have shared and
you will realised that our
meeting and time together
could have only been
because of love.

Falling for petals

<u>Over You</u>

ever since the day
you walked away
i was over you.
i never looked back
even though i still remember.

my eyes might have leaked
but my soul was never weak.

i have never been tempted
to rekindle the fire
but every now and again
my knees still get weak
at the thought of you.

i have been over you
for a long time now
but in my dreams you still
make my heart leap,
i still quiver at the mention
of your name
and the image of your unspoiled
beauty still gets me jittery.

lonely nights still evoke
fond memories of you and me,
and the sound of those love songs
we use to play
still rings in the halls of my ears.
ever since that day,

r. A. bentinck

you walked out
of my life
i was over you.
i never looked back
even though i still remember
so much about you and me.

Falling for petals

The Petal Philosophy

some roses should never be picked
by inexperienced hands
with an insensitive heart.

they require
that delicate touch
of gentle fingers
and a tender heart
that some pickers
don't possess at the moment.

some are quick to be
seduced by the beauty
of her petal without
understanding and appreciating
the time and care it took
for her irresistible beauty
to shine so radiantly.

some gardens are not deserving
of a certain type of rose.

their shabby fencing
allow intruders.
their neglect allow
weeds to grow and dominate,

and their level of ignorance
blind them from seeing
what gems

r. A. bentinck

they have growing
among the stifling weeds.

just because you can pick
a rose doesn't mean
you should.
some roses bloom best
on the trees and in
the garden you discovered them.

A Ballad for the Broken (to My Sisters with Love)

she is an earth angel
who carries her natural beauty
with effortless simplicity.
but they have hurt her
so she doesn't trust love
anymore.

sister, please come home to love.

someone smeared her innocence
in her tender years and squashed
the petals of her fragile flower.
now she is on a hurting mission
and
she will take no prisoners.
she really doesn't care about love
and she doesn't want to be loved.

sister, please come home to love.

her trust in men has been
compromised
now she finds it hard to believe
and give in to her natural feelings.
her sexiness causes the thermometer
to explode but her heart
is cold as below zero.
sister, please come home to love.
her hands are soft as a baby's cheek

but her caress is as hard
as greenheart wood.
she has been badly treated
and repeatedly molested
now she finds it too complex
to trust her tenderness.
sister, please come home to love.

her gentle tears struggle
to penetrate her steely eyes.
she has cried a thousand tears before
in silent places but always manages
to fake a smile for the world.
she is hurting daily
in places she rather not tell.

sister, please come home to love.

i stand in her pain
for a fleeting moment
and empathy hurts like a bitch!
but she carries this hurt daily
and often the painful memories
come calling, softly but brutally.

sister, please come home to love.
if my unrepentant brothers can
only see the deep and long-lasting
scars and pains they subjected
our sisters to
will they ever change?
will they rearrange their foolish ways?

Falling for petals

will they ever open their eyes
to see?

brothers let's please help
our sisters come home to love.
please

r. A. bentinck

Conflicted

you give me reasons
to leave on countless
occasions,
you showed me
the door so many times before,

you told me not
to hang around,
you said we were becoming
fading memories.

so now that i am leaving
you now want me
to stay.

you are standing in my way
begging me not to go.
i am confused.

you took away
our reasons
to try a little harder,

you took away
our reasons
to hope against hope.

you stiletto punctured
my already fragile heart.
and now

Falling for petals

you want me
to stay.

you gradually destroyed us.
you stripped our relationship
of its humanness.
now i have built up
the courage
to walk away
you are pleading with me
not to go.

it is with a heavy heart
that i close this chapter
in our book
as i leave tracks
of my teardrops
to dry in the process
of time.

r. A. bentinck

The Long Kiss Goodbye

you can never truly
prepare for them,
those goodbyes.

sometimes
you can sense them coming.
others
catch you by surprise.

despite what form they take
they always leave footprints
of gloom and trails of regrets.

you can never really tell
who comes for
a short time,
a long time
or a lifetime.

there is no manuscript
that fits all our relationships
in any uniform and consistent way.

some relationships
are meant to be short
when we wish them
to be long,

others are meant
to be steamy and fiery

Falling for petals

leaving us breathless,
wondering
where did that come from?
some outlast our tough times
and endless sorrows,
while others are unassuming
yet dependable.

but there comes a time
when we are meant to say
goodbye to some relationships.

but we hang on,
drag on,
prolong and extend
those long goodbye kisses.

when a relationship has
served its purpose let go.

you must avoid
the temptations
to prolong
those long goodbye kisses.

r. A. bentinck

<u>Try Again</u>

no, it's not an exaggeration.
it was mental hell!

it was torturous,
it drained me
of my lifeblood
it left me weak and disheveled.

now she is knocking
on my backdoor
appealing
to my tender side
and
flashing her irresistible smile
asking me for another chance.

my knees might be weak
and my heart is forgiving
but
the memories of my scars
and bruises
would not let me give in.

i can still see the tenderness
in her enchanting eyes
but the image
of her walking away
is still fresh
like it was just yesterday.
i mentally slapped myself

Falling for petals

back to my sense and i swiftly
avoid eye contact.

giving her another try
will be dangerous
to my mental health
and peace of mind.
i won't do it!

r. A. bentinck

Indelible Hurt

be careful of the words
you wield
they can inflict wounds
like a samurai's sword.

some of which are
destructively invisible.

idle words
in anger and frustration,
can destroy trust,

kill spontaneity,
injure self-belief,
and burn the edges
of a blooming rose petal.

words sling in anger
can hurt in ways
that cannot be put in words.

they can destroy
the gains you have made
together,

they can force
an uncomfortable silence
in a good relationship.

take the time

Falling for petals

to taste your words
before you serve them
to the ones you love.

r. A. bentinck

COVID-19 (a lover's regrets)

i cleaned all i can clean.
i slept till i am tired of sleeping.
i run out of things
and recipe to cook.

i binge-watched tv
till i am tired.
my favourite songs have grown tired
of the replaying.

i've repeatedly looked through all
the windows in my apartment
and i can count all the leaves
on the blossoming trees
in my rose garden.
now i can no longer evade these
fierce thoughts that have been
pursuing me around
my desolate apartment
these past few days.

my avoidance strategies
no longer work.

i voluntarily resigned to the fact
that i must acknowledge
my ultimate truth.
i replay the suffering
and the pains i caused her,
i retrace every foolish choice

Falling for petals

i made that induced pain.
i can recall the tears she wept
and i relive the pain
in her eyes again and again.

her joy-filled laughter resounds
in my mind,
her indelible smile
is still outstanding
in my fond remembrances.

her familiar smell still survived
in the isles of my nostrils,
and her infectious personality
still, embrace me affectionately.

why did i forsake her?
my guilt-filled thoughts enquired.
why?
why didn't i treat her like
the queen she is?

why didn't i spend more quality
with her?
why?

questions crowded my head
like a determined detective
seeking to break a mystery.

i cracked under pressure
of an unceasing bombardment

of specific questions
and my eyes leaked
from the unbearable squeeze.

i choked
on the strangling emotions
and curled up like an innocent baby
in the coldness of my loneliness.

i am too depleted
to resist anymore.

amid these 14 days
of quarantine, i wilt under
the pressures of crushing,
and
remorseful memories.

Falling for petals

Courage-less

in my silent moments,
there is so much i want
to say, but
my overthinking mind
silences my courage.

i want to tell you
that i know i was wrong
on so many issues
and so many of my actions
was guided by selfish gains.

in silence, i would say to you
how much you mean to me
and how much i appreciate
all the simple but
profound things you do
for me.

i have had so many conversations
in my head with you,
but in reality
i lose the courage to speak
those same words
to your listening ear.

my acculturated macho qualities
won't permit me
to be that 'weak.'
i stand before you

r. A. bentinck

with a haughty chest
but a guilt-riddled mind
just because there is
a soft side inside of me
just for you.

in my quiet moments,
there is so much
that dominates my thoughts

but my overactive imagination
slaughters my courage
to speak them out loud
for you to hear.

Falling for petals

My Soft-Spoken Princess

there is always a sad tone
in her voice, if i call home
to say i'll be running
a little late.

there is always
a gloomy countenance that
cloaks her every time
i have to go out with my friends.

this the same soft-spoken,
heart-stealing,
fun-filled,
ever-smiling woman
i fell in love with years ago.

but now that things
have changed over the years
i honestly don't know what and
who i am going
to come home to anymore.

coming home late means
i am subjected
to detective like examinations.

there are checks for
lipstick stains,
scratch marks and
strange perfume trails.

r. A. bentinck

when it all started
i misread her insecurities
and fears as simply her way
of loving me
madly.

now it's weighing down
my psyche and taking a toll
on our relationship
and daily life.

don't misread me.
i love this woman dearly,
but i can feel the courage
and strength to hold on
slipping beneath my feet.

the temptation fields are
ripe and ready for the picking.
on my daily grind, i am presented
with a plethora of options.
it's so easy for me to give in
but i don't.

she makes insensitive privacy request.
she often was complete access
to all the private contents of
my phone. its the only way
i can prove my innocence
and appease her unrelenting nagging.

her excuse is always:

Falling for petals

babe, i am afraid,
i don't lose you,
you mean the world to me.

in the early days, i dealt
with these frequent occurrences
with so much
understanding and composure
but now i'm losing my grip
and it shows on my face
and my emotional posture.

i don't know how much longer
i can endure this barrage at home
and still navigate
the less stressful temptations
on the road unscathed.
i truly don't know.

r. A. bentinck

Love's Aftertaste.

moving on wasn't
the toughest of challenges.
losing the pleasant aftertaste
of her love has been
the most arduous task.

wherever you may be
at this time i hope these
lines can find their way
to your heart and speak to you.

my days are not the same,
the moonlight doesn't shine
as brilliant with not by my side,

the lyrics of our favourite love songs
have converted from cheerful
to melancholy,

the flowers in the garden
don't have that affectionate fragrance
like they use to.
they use to smell sweeter
when you were here with me.

the love birds outside
my window doesn't sing
that melodious song anymore.

every girl that comes into

Falling for petals

my life gets measured
by the towering standards, you left.

i know its unjust to them
but i can't seem to lose
the aroma of your love.

i have done all i can do
and nothing seems to take away
the taste of your love.

i thought given time
i would have overcome it all,
but time doesn't kill
the savory flavours you leave
in my life.

r. A. bentinck

Travelling

i have travelled
the world and i always
find a way to treasure
the memories of sights seen.

i have journeyed
to varying places and
brought back rare souvenirs.

now
here i am
travelling through
your memories and
the things we once treasured
pains me.

and i have learned that
a broken heart
don't make a good souvenir.

remembering how it
uses to be don't make me happy.

i travel through
our indelible memories
and they don't make me smile
like they use to.

Falling for petals

One More Time

will i ever forget you?
i don't think so.

you have
in subtle ways
left some indelible marks
in my life.

you have
walked with me
through some of my deepest
and most treacherous valleys,

you have been my shelter
throughout so many
rainy days,
you have been my voice
of reasoning
and constant support
when all else failed,

you stayed with me
in the numerous difficult days
and the countless nights
that never wanted to end.

now here we are
at the crossroads
of it all
and though

r. A. bentinck

the tears flow,
the heart aches,
the memories
come flooding in,
we both know how
this will conclude.

so we held each other
one more time,
we kissed each other
one more time,
we looked into each other's eyes
one more time.

and though the emotions
that engulf us are so strong
we know it's only logical
that we go our separate ways.

apart now,
but never forgotten.
separated inflected
by time and circumstances.
but the memories
that unite us
will never be erased.

Falling for petals

Of Thorns and Roses

beautiful petals
is not a guarantee
of a sweet-smelling rose.

some roses are best
appreciated from a distance.

some roses are not
very welcoming
to the hummingbirds
and the bees.
what makes you think
your reality would be
different?

intimidating thorns
doesn't mean you cannot
get to the sweet rose
they protect.
the more valuable
the rose the fiercer
the thorns.

some of the most
exceptional roses
can be found
blooming among
the most intimidating thorns
for good reasons.
each rose has its own story

r. A. bentinck

and for some the thorns
are there for more than
protection.
they are the symbols
of the extra value
nature places on some
of her most priceless gems.

Falling for petals

Reaping Stupidity

for my machoness
and immaturity
all i have left are
bittersweet memories.

in my quiet moments
i hear echoes
of your angelic voice
and the gush of sadness
slaps me in the face
reminding me
of my once shallowness.

i walk down lonely avenues
repeatedly
trying to recapture
the magic we once shared.
with my head in the clouds
i can hear your footsteps
next to me
and then the happy couple
that just pasted by me
snaps me back to reality.

i am just a lonely fool
who is now a junkie
on yesterday's sweet memories.

my once tender nights
are not so gentle anymore

and peaceful sleep has now
become my regular wishful thinking.

sometimes we make
the hardest of bed
and then complain
when we must sleep
alone in them
all alone.

Falling for petals

No Limits

the sky was not
the limit.
i did anything
for her
and i will still do.

i felt love
and
i called it love.

she said she felt
nothing
and she called it
a thing we shared.

despite the shards of glass
she threw in my path
my warm heart
was a magnet
to her steel heart.

despite
the poison-tipped arrows
she constantly shot
to my heart,
i bleed and recovered
over and over again.

i have survived the sustained
assault of her mean

and unfriendly words
disguised as honesty.

in my world
she was never constrained
by limitations
she was too important for that.

but
in her world
i was the convenience that
kept on giving
and she had no problem
with accepting.

Falling for petals

My Weakness

i worked hard
to develop my mental toughness
and I have worked doubly hard
to maintain it.

mama always use
to say to me…
it's the one you least expect son,
she is the one who is
going to break down
your toughness,
bring you to your knees
and increase
your level of stupidity.

i use to smile
at my mother
every time she makes
that statement
and respectfully
hold my overconfident tongue
and smartass reply.

today i'm staring at
the prototype
my mother spoke about.

i hate it when my mother
is right about certain things!
here i am with this damsel

that's leading me by
my nose through hell
but i love it.
what the…!
the way she treats me
my friends call me weak,
my family is constantly
asking me what did she
give me to eat.

i was told my
stupidity meter
is off the reading scale.

my ex told me
one day that
this girl is using me
like her doormat
and as much as she wants
to celebrate she pity me.
whatever they are
talking about
i am oblivious it.

but
something about
the way
this girl
treats me
makes the people who love me
feel immense sadness for me.

Falling for petals

Incapably

i would have given her
the best of me.

i would have sacrificed
more than was needed
just to keep her happy

but still she never
seemed interested
in reciprocating the love.

she claimed not
to know what love is,
and was never capable
of loving
and will never
be able to love…
EVER.

she is still possessed
by the memories
of countless abuse.

i am being robbed
of a wonderful woman
just because misguided men
took advantage of an angel
in her youthful years.

r. A. bentinck

Disbelief

are these your hands
now holding mine?

somehow
in your distance past
i never met
the stringent criteria
you set for those
who earned your love.

are those your desiring eyes
staring into mine?
somehow long ago
i was never
afforded the opportunity
to look into them before.
what changed?

when did i cross your mind?
what changed for you?
did you lower
your highfalutin standards
or
did you realised
you were too blind
to see the real me before?

what changed?
i am curious.

Falling for petals

Who Else?

you are full *of shit,*
you know that?

who else is gonna
tolerate you and
your countless mood swings?

just because i stood
by you all these years
don't mean i can't
walkout and leave now!

don't take me for granted!

who else
will understand you
as i do?
tell me, please.

get your shit together,
and get it together quick!

i sat there in
the barrage of corrections
without saying a single word
because i knew she was right,
just like so many times before.

who else
would have tolerated you

r. A. bentinck

with your shit after
so many years?
please tell me, babe.

Falling for petals

Move On

it's so easy
for everyone
to say:

move on,
get over her,
find someone new,
time will heal it all.

they are not standing
in my place.

they are not in my shoe.
they haven't walked
a kilometer in it either.

they are not there
when her memories are
too much to bear,
so i silently call her name.

somehow i foolishly thought
that with time
i would have gotten
over it all.

i was dead wrong!

now,
here i am once again

r. A. bentinck

buckling under
the cutting pains
of her abiding memories
activated by
the dj on the radio
who is playing
an extended segment
of her favorite love songs.

i am still battling unexplained
sleepless nights.

i am still randomly
recollecting cherished memories
and rereading old love notes.

i have slowly become
both a victim and a prisoner
to her abiding sweetness.

Falling for petals

Moments in Time

with you, i have come
to appreciate
the importance of savouring
each moment in time.

one moment
we are all wrapped up
in the bosom of smiles
and joy-filled laughter,

and in the wink of an eye
we are battling with
your resurfacing grotesque memories.

one moment
your eyes are bright
with excitement
and your words
filled with hopeful optimism

and in a flash
the moments that follow
we are battling
to swim against
the tsunami-like waves
of your hopelessness
and sorrows.

these frequent fluctuating moments
are a threat to the beauty

and the lifeblood
of our relationship.

as we continue to struggle
with your hurt filled daemons
daily
i have gradually learned
to be grateful for
the beautiful moments
in time
that we share.

i have learned
to treasure,
and enjoy
those elusive moments
of genuine love,
and excitement,

because
i can never telegraph
when it will all metaphor
for the worst
just because your memories
drags you back to that painful past.

Falling for petals

Pearls of Hurt

she wore her past hurt
and shortcomings like
expensive pearls.

she polishes
and shows them off
for those who want
to pay attention to see.

she protects her actions
with plausible excuses
and logical reasoning.

she makes it harder
to love the hurt away.

she blames the world
she lives in
claiming
she doesn't belong in it.

she blames her abusers,
she blames her circumstances.

she focuses so much
on blaming
that she cannot see
the solutions sitting
on her lap.
she wears her past hurt

r. A. bentinck

and shortcomings like
expensive pearls
and

no matter what people say
she continues to treasure
them in unhealthy ways
which makes it complicated
to love her
in the traditional way.

Falling for petals

From One Man to All Women

it's not that we
don't love you anymore
we have so much
going on in our heads
that we are yet to comprehend.

don't be too quick to judge.

it's not that we are avoiding
speaking to you

some of us don't know
where to start,

some of us are too macho
to admit that we are dealing
with difficult
and unexplainable things.

some of us are too scared
to share and some of us
know you have the memory
of an elephant.

give us space, please
don't make it about you always.

no,
she is not another woman
she is a platonic friend.

r. A. bentinck

i hope you know
men are allowed to have
those platonic relationships
right?
don't paint us all with the
same judgemental brush.
some of us are dealing
with deep hurt
just like you.

Perceived Value

i am the fly
in your sweetened milk
but
the honey
in her daily coffee.

to you
i am
the stressed wrinkles
on your pretty face
but
to her
i am

the joy-filled smile
that glows on
her lively face.
to you
i am your
hard and
uncomfortable mattress-
sleep doesn't come easily,

but
i to her
i am
the gel memory foam mattress-
peaceful sleep comes with
natural ease.
isn't it interesting

r. A. bentinck

how you can be seen
and valued differently
by the people who
share chapters of
your life.

Falling for petals

One Night

it was one of those
unexpected meeting
that brought with it
a serenading connection.

the casual introduction
by a mutual friend,
the seductive musical setting
and a vibrational vibing
that led
to unanticipated goodness.

one night,
one glance,
one dance,
one kiss,
one embrace,
one word,

and the emotions
came in like
the welcoming tides.

and after many spoken words,
countless unspoken thoughts
the realisation gradually dawned.

something was suddenly blooming.
and anyone who had eyes
was a spectator

to this theatre
of a burgeoning fairytale.

her natural vibes
and serene eyes.
her silk sensuality
and fragrance heaven,
all created
a cherry daiquiri
worth sipping.

one night,
one vibe,
one musical connection
and lots of mutual desires
lit a fire in their souls

and created a connected
they didn't
plan for
or expected.

but they both
surrendered
to its siren calling.

Flying in the Rain

she asked me
to fly with broken wings,
in torrential rain.

i spread my wings
too wide
just to shield her from
her stormy weathers,

i cradled her
with my feathers
on cold and windy days,

i fed her love
even when she refused
to eat,
as i stand here
contemplating
the torrid journey ahead
i know i will make it.

i have flown this route
before
but not with broken wings
and inclement weather like this.

r. A. bentinck

<u>Choosing My Memories</u>

there is a lot about you
that i can remember
but
i choose to remember
the way you love me.

there is so much
about you to celebrate
but i choose to celebrate
your mischievous smile
and the light
in your childish eyes
when you are happy
on a deeper level.

i choose to remember
the warmth of your
unforgettable touch
and
your tender laughter
that echoes in the hallway
of my ear.

you've left me
with so many memories
but i choose to remember
the ones that are always
sweet for you and me.

Falling for petals

Split Seconds

resurrected memories.
the turning back
of time.

the thought
of your lips
touching mine,
and
just like that
you are dominating
my mind
again.

i've liberated myself
from
your chains
the ones that
once enslaved
and
blinded me.

i've scrubbed and vacuum
my mind
of your residue recollection.

yet here i am
once again
managing the presence
of your pesky memories.
in the sanctuary

r. A. bentinck

of my at ease mind
she always finds ways
to make her presence felt
with memories
i thought i set free.

About The Author

Randy Abubakar Bentinck

R. A. Bentinck is the author of 7 other poetry books, including *Of all the Lilies, Underneath the Poetry with My Girl, Underneath the Poetry and Bad Girl Stricken, and Seduced.* He presently lives in Georgetown, Guyana. His latest release, *The Flaws in Our Teens* was a #1 bestseller in the Being a Teen new release category of on Amazon.

He is also an Educator and Artist who is presently focusing on his self-publishing business while tutoring part-time at the E.R. Burrowes School of Art as a painting and drawing Tutor.

r. A. bentinck

Bentinck is a graduate of the University of Guyana with a B. A. Degree in Fine Arts (Hons) and a Diploma in Education (Administration).